The First
100
Words

The First
100
Words

Stephen Parrish
with the editors of *The Lascaux Review*

L SCAUX
B O O K S

ISBN: 978-1-7344966-0-4

Cover design by Wendy Russ.

Lascaux Books
www.lascauxbooks.com

Acknowledgments

Editors and friends of *The Lascaux Review* who said mean things about *The First 100 Words*, and thus made it better, include Kevin Aicher, Diana Blackwood, Marissa Glover, Alissa Grosso, Michelle Hickman, Sarah Hina, Lois P. Jones, Sarah Laurenson, Laurel Miram, Wendy Russ, Sarah Specht, Trevy Thomas, and Jennifer Zobair.

The Lascaux Review appears online at lascauxreview.com. Proceeds from *The First 100 Words* are dedicated to operating the review.

Contents

Introduction

The first 100 words of your manuscript are as important as all the words that follow. They comprise a first impression. They set the tone and introduce your writing style. If poorly chosen, they may be the only words an editor reads. The purpose of *The First 100 Words* is to share one editorial staff's insights into that narrow literary domain, to chart the pitfalls and headlong plunges that inspire frontline readers to reject manuscripts, often without bothering to finish them.

It may seem unfair. After all, doesn't your entire submission deserve attention? Think of the first 100 words as an abbreviated job application. If you make grammatical errors in your cover letter, if you employ a bizarre format, the manager who makes the hiring decision probably won't bother to call your references. She has other applicants to interview. The volume of submissions to literary journals is so high, editors don't have time to read everything. If you want them to keep reading your submission, give them sufficient reason in the first 100 words.

We've been reading unsolicited submissions at *The Lascaux Review* for fourteen years, and what follows are the mistakes—as we see them—that appear again and again in manuscripts. Mistakes that make otherwise talented writers look like amateurs, and yet are easily avoided. We frown upon lists of "don'ts" as much as anyone, but we think it's valuable to know what's on those lists, even if only to dodge the gatekeepers.

We intend to revise this book as necessary, and we invite everyone within earshot to participate. Send your constructive criticism, your rules, arguments, and examples, to lascauxreview@gmail.com. If we use your input we'll add your name to the acknowledgments when the next edition comes out.

Meanwhile pay attention. Maybe your stories, poems, and essays aren't being rejected after all. Maybe only the first 100 words are to blame.

Before We Start

While sharing an early draft of this book we got a peek at the broad spectrum of literary taste, revealed especially by opposing opinions about the writing examples we chose to include. One reader's literary monument is another's object of derision. Consider the opening paragraph of *A Farewell to Arms* by Ernest Hemingway:

In the late summer of that year we lived in a house in a village that looked across the river and the plain to the mountains. In the bed of the river there were pebbles and boulders, dry and white in the sun, and the water was clear and swiftly moving and blue in the channels. Troops went by the house and down the road and the dust they raised powdered the leaves of the trees. The trunks of the trees too were dusty and the leaves fell early that year and we saw the troops marching along the road and the dust rising and leaves, stirred by the breeze, falling and the soldiers marching and afterward the road bare and white except for the leaves.

It consists of 126 words, only one of which has three syllables. Some readers consider it to be a pillar in the canon of American literature. Others cringe when they read it. There is no right answer.

To quote Richard Bach, *Everything in this book may be wrong.*

Give Us Reason to Care

The absence of a reason to care is the most common problem we see in creative writing. Like all readers, editors want something to care about, as early in the piece as possible. In the first line, if possible, and certainly in the first 100 words. The thing to care about is usually a protagonist, but editors are open-minded; it could be a villain or even an inanimate object. We care, in general, because an emotion is piqued. The emotion can be pity, curiosity, fear, even humor—anything that makes us *feel* enough to keep reading.

In "The Canterville Ghost" it's the ghost we come to know best and to pity, but in the first 100 words it's someone else who gives us something, right away, to care about. The effect can be subtle, as you'll see. Here's the opening sentence:

When Mr. Hiram B. Otis, the American Minister, bought Canterville Chase, every one told him he was doing a very foolish thing, as there was no doubt at all that the place was haunted.

This opening is effective for several reasons, not least of which is that it intrigues us; we want to know the circumstances of the haunting. But look at poor Mr. Hiram B. Otis. We're immediately, if subconsciously, concerned about him, because he has stepped into an uncomfortable situation merely by purchasing a house. Even his name evokes pity. Oscar Wilde makes us care, and it only takes him 34 words to do it.

You don't have to create a cataclysmic event and make characters suffer; doing so may well backfire. You only have to provide sufficient reason to continue reading. To round out the lesson, here are the first 106 words:

When Mr. Hiram B. Otis, the American Minister, bought Canterville Chase, every one told him he was doing a very foolish thing, as there was no doubt at all that the place was haunted. Indeed, Lord Canterville himself, who was a man of the most punctilious honour, had felt it his duty to mention the fact to Mr. Otis when they came to discuss terms.

"We have not cared to live in the place ourselves," said Lord Canterville, "since my grandaunt, the Dowager Duchess of Bolton, was frightened into a fit, from which she never really recovered, by two skeleton hands being placed on her shoulders..."

Who can fail to care about that? Here's another example, from "The Necklace" by Guy de Maupassant:

She was one of those pretty and charming girls who are sometimes, as if by a mistake of destiny, born in a family of clerks. She had no dowry, no expectations, no means of being known, understood, loved, wedded by any rich and distinguished man; and she let herself be married to a little clerk at the Ministry of Public Instruction.

Poor thing! Of course, her life could be much worse, but the protagonist could be any of us, because at some time or another we all feel sorry for ourselves. Note it's insufficient merely to list a character's issues; we need something specific to pity. The wonderful detail that concludes this 61-word opening, in contrast to the generalities preceding it, is that she didn't just marry a clerk, she married one at the Ministry of Public Instruction, of all places. Her life is over. Speaking of which:

When Miss Emily Grierson died, our whole town went to her funeral: the men through a sort of respectful affection for a fallen monument, the women mostly out of curiosity to see the inside of her house, which no one save an old manservant—a combined gardener and cook—had seen in at least ten years.

Here we care because we're curious. We want to know all about Miss Emily Grierson, why she's a fallen monument, what it is she fell from. And frankly it isn't just women who want to see the inside of her house. In these first 56 words

Faulkner creates a mysterious world, one we're going to keep reading to explore. And as those of you who are familiar with "A Rose for Emily" can attest, the time spent reading isn't wasted.

Curiosity is also the focus of the opening of "The Odd Job" by Ian Anderson:

I'm sitting at the kitchen table with my Saturday afternoon tea when Georgie comes in through the back.

He's talking even before he closes the door. "Wait until you hear this one. You are not going to believe this one."

Naturally we, the editors, will keep reading to learn what "this one" is all about.

We'll give Henry James a few extra words to get his job done. Here are the first 143 of "The Turn of the Screw."

The story had held us, round the fire, sufficiently breathless, but except the obvious remark that it was gruesome, as, on Christmas Eve in an old house, a strange tale should essentially be, I remember no comment uttered till somebody happened to say that it was the only case he had met in which such a visitation had fallen on a child. The case, I may mention, was that of an apparition in just such an old house as had gathered us for the occasion—an appearance, of a dreadful kind, to a little boy sleeping in the room with his mother and waking her up in the terror of it; waking her not to dissipate his dread and soothe him to sleep again, but to encounter also, herself, before she had succeeded in doing so, the same sight that had shaken him.

The funny thing about horror is, we always look in the basement even though they tell us not to. *The Scare* is why *We Care.* The opening above may seem wordy. But horror has to creep up on you, and we think Mr. James found the right pace.

In the first 139 words of *Wild Seed* by Octavia Butler we don't have to be told when or where the story takes place, nor do we have to be asked twice to follow the author's lead:

Doro discovered the woman by accident when he went to see what was left of one of his seed villages. The village was a comfortable mud-walled place surrounded by grasslands and scattered trees. But Doro realized even before he reached it that its people were gone. Slavers had been to it before him. With their guns and their greed, they had undone in a few hours the work of a thousand years. Those villagers they had not herded away, they had slaughtered. Doro found human bones, hair, bits of desiccated flesh missed by scavengers. He stood over a very small skeleton—the bones of a child—and wondered where the survivors had been taken. Which country or New World colony? How far would he have to travel to find the remnants of what had been a healthy, vigorous people?

7

Okay, now a change of direction. This is a story published in *The Lascaux Review*, about a woman who wishes to return to her home planet. It's by Alice Hatcher, it's called "Mr. Chips and the Mango-Tango Mother Ship," and it's here: lascauxreview.com/mr-chips-mother-ship. Read it and decide for yourself whether the protagonist is nuts. Following are the first 108 words:

Marylou was breaking it off with the human race once and for all, leaving the whole miserable lot for good, and this time for real. The whole thing had been a mistake from the start, an ill-conceived exploratory mission to gather data about evolutionary dead ends. High time had come to drive out to the desert, where she'd been deposited so many years ago—thirty-five, not that there was any point in counting, since no one had ever given a cold crap about her birthday or bothered to determine its exact date—to meet the Mother Ship and shake off the dust of this wreck of a planet.

We can't leave this section without providing an example of 100 words that don't get the job done. Unfortunately it's more representative of what we find in the slush. (This and all other examples provided without attribution are fabricated for instructional purposes. No writers were harmed in the making of this book.) Let's use a creative nonfiction example this time:

I hid under the covers and tried to think of a reason to get out of bed. The TV was still on, left on from the night before, and "Amber" was leading an exercise routine in her tights. I found her over-the-top enthusiasm uninspiring. It made no dent at all in my depression. The curtains were open and the unwelcome sun shined loudly in my face. I turned away from it and stared at the wall. My mother was calling my siblings to breakfast, and I could already smell the bacon and toast. I wondered if she would bother to check in on me.

Here the author may argue she has created pitiable circumstances. The problem is, she hasn't given us anything to care about, because unlike the miserable girl married to a clerk in the Ministry of Public Instruction, this character doesn't share the specific cause of his apathy. Don't tell us your protagonist deserves compassion, show us. But we're getting ahead of ourselves. We are in an impetuous mood.

*

Avoid introducing characters with personal pronouns and providing names later, even one sentence later. For example:

She dressed in a rush Monday morning. Tammy had an interview for her dream job.

Switch the pronoun with the name in these two sentences and see how much better it sounds. The sooner we know a character's name, the sooner we can become comfortable with her.

Tammy dressed in a rush Monday morning. She had an interview for her dream job, and the alarm clock told her the only way she'd catch the bus was by leaping out the bedroom window.

But now look what we've done. We've added a reason to care about Tammy. Sometimes you have to sit on your characters to make them uncomfortable.

There are countless ways to make readers care in the first 100 words. No doubt you can come up with examples of your own, stories you've read that hooked you in the first few sentences. It doesn't matter how you do it, as long as you do it. Because if you, the writer, don't appear to care, the moment you begin writing, don't expect us, the editors, to care either, the moment we begin reading.

And here's a secret: editors who get hooked during the first 100 words will forgive mistakes that follow. On the other hand, if they feel you've dragged them unwillingly into a story, they'll search like Diogenes for reasons to reject it.

Show, Don't Tell

During the past ten years or so quite a bit of push-back against "Show, Don't Tell" has appeared in the how-to literature. Pay no attention to it. Of course there are times you must "Tell, Don't Show," for instance when transitioning or summarizing:

After the fight with Tom, Cindy spent a week in her lakeside cabin, wondering whether she should continue to see him, whether the relationship would survive.

Nothing wrong with this. We don't need to see Cindy travel to the cabin, park her car, pace the floor, mumble to herself, drink whiskey to excess. The "Show, Don't Tell" rule applies when we *should* see such things. Compare:

Cindy was angry.

with:

Cindy slammed the door.

If you keep this one example in mind while you write, you'll never break the "Show, Don't Tell" rule. You might even get published; we are in an optimistic mood.

In the opening paragraph of *How We Fight For Our Lives* Saeed Jones paints a vivid picture of 90 degree heat:

The waxy-faced weatherman on Channel 8 said we had been above 90 degrees for ten days in a row. Day after day of my T-shirt sticking to the sweat on my lower back, the smell of insect repellant gone slick with sunscreen, the air droning with the hum of cicadas, dead yellow grass crackling under every footstep, asphalt bubbling on the roads. It didn't occur to me to be nervous about the occasional wall of white smoke on the horizon that summer. Everything already looked like it was scorched, dead, or well on its way.

A less experienced writer might have opened the piece with "It was hot."

When talking about the first 100 words we're mostly talking about prose, of course. In poetry we zero in on the first line or stanza. If you don't grab the reader there, the odds of doing so thereafter fall precipitously. Poetry provides good examples of showing-not-telling because poets learned the rule long before the rest of us. The first four stanzas of "At a Truck Stop on Highway 124" by Andrea Witzke Slot lack explicit answers to the questions What is the poet trying to

tell us? and Why? Read the poem at lascauxreview.com/
truck-stop-on-highway-124 and decide for yourself.

The odor of stale hotdogs coils
around this truck stop of quiet men
who sit with faces bowed, bath kits
in laps, fair-like tickets in hand.

We take turns flipping through pages
of four-year-old Time magazines,
setting one down, picking up another,
sharing the sensation one has when

returning to land after days on a ship,
the road still gravelling under our feet,
the car radio still humming in our ears,
the speed unnoticed, natural, easy.

Beyond my rocking body, outside
the window, my hobbled car is hunched
in front of their monster-sized trucks.
Diesel fumes rise in the August heat.

There's so much wonderful about this poem—the appeal to
senses, the metaphors, the subtle anthropomorphism—but
note the absence of telling. Now read the first twelve lines
of a poem by Janna Vought:

Mosaic memory,
intoxication, swallowed swigs
of beer, Marijuana haze,
unsteady, leaden head, sweltering
dance, tribal beat, sweat
veins, eyes watching,
directionless, blue shirted
boy fading in
and out, metallic voice,
words, ruthless, ravenous,
unhinged beast, friend no
more, heavy hand

What do you think the poem is about? The poet doesn't tell us explicitly, except in the title: "Fragments of My Rape" (lascauxreview.com/fragments-of-my-rape). It continues in the same disturbing, stream-of-consciousness vein. Read those twelve lines again; do the poet's words impact you differently now that you know the title?

We've been ignoring someone who will roll over in his grave if we don't mention him. If you didn't know the title of the following poem by Shakespeare was "Winter" you'd nevertheless comprehend the subject. But isn't comprehension more engaging when you aren't told how to do it? We think so, except when necessary, as in the Janna Vought example above. We think poems like the following get the job done without an explanatory label. If anything, their titles should contribute to Showing, should take advantage of an opportunity to share additional insight, which the word "Winter" doesn't. (And now Shakespeare *is* rolling over in his grave.)

When icicles hang by the wall,
And Dick the shepherd blows his nail,
And Tom bears logs into the hall,
And milk comes frozen home in pail,
When blood is nipp'd and ways be foul,
Then nightly sings the staring owl,
Tu-whit; Tu-who, a merry note,
While greasy Joan doth keel the pot.

When all aloud the wind doth blow,
And coughing drowns the parson's saw,
And birds sit brooding in the snow,
And Marion's nose looks red and raw,
When roasted crabs hiss in the bowl,
Then nightly sings the staring owl,
Tu-whit; Tu-who, a merry note,
While greasy Joan doth keel the pot.

Finally, as an exercise, ask yourself why Hemingway changed the title of one of his stories from "The Horns of the Bull" to "The Capital of the World" when he anthologized it. Find a copy and read it. We think you'll agree the change improves the reading experience.

*

Back to our earlier example, don't make the mistake of saying

Cindy was angry. She slammed the door.

This is both telling and showing when you only need to show. If you begin your story with Cindy being angry rather than Cindy slamming the door, you'd better have another hook up your sleeve. Like Cindy's house is haunted. Or Cindy wants to return to her home planet. If your story opens under mundane circumstances, with everything interesting yet to come—and many great stories do just that—you might in fact want to show your protagonist driving to the cabin, mumbling to herself, and pouring Scotch down her throat.

But wait a minute. Why is it now Scotch rather than mere whiskey?

Provide Appropriate Detail

Aspiring poets and writers have trouble with this one, and it's easy to understand why. How much detail is enough? The answer is, it's a matter of experience. Follow Anne Lamott's advice to describe what you can see through a one-inch picture frame—and don't shift the frame around to get everything in. Let's begin with this creature:

After the fight with Tom, Cindy drove her Ford Escort down Highway 77 to her cabin adjacent to Stillwater Lake. She parked between two Douglas Firs, in fact a foot or so closer to one than the other, and consequently had difficulty exiting the car. As she squeezed her way out she thought, "This is what it must feel like when accident victims are extracted from their vehicles." She strolled down the flagstone path and entered the rustic old cabin through the squeaky front door. Inside she paced the oak parquet floor, uttering expressions of exasperation: "Why do I allow Tom to treat me this way?" all the while tossing shots down her throat. Not the cheap stuff, ten-year-old Scotch in fact, with a small dash of water to lessen the bite.

Don't shake your head. This kind of stuff shows up in the slush *all the time*. "Provide details" doesn't mean provide *all* the details. It means provide just enough. Having said that, if you must err on one side or another, err on the side of too much. We may not care that the cabin is on Stillwater Lake, but we won't reject you for sharing the information, and it's easier to cut than to create.

Why is this hard? When you read passages like the one above you immediately recognize that they contain too much detail. Yet in your own work it doesn't seem that way; you feel you must paint pictures for readers, to keep their attention. And that's where you go wrong.

The reason watching TV is passive is because the screen paints all the pictures for you; it leaves nothing to the imagination. Reading is active, relatively speaking, because your brain must do some work, in fact quite a lot of work. And if it doesn't—if the writer has illustrated everything for you— you become bored and turn on the TV. Readers of prose and poetry must be engaged, not lectured. Consider the following description of a tumbledown house:

One of the shutters was broken and dangled crookedly, and dandelions populated the yard.

You immediately create a picture of the house in your head. It doesn't matter if the house is the same as the one in our head, only that readers understand—are shown—it's a tumbledown house. Now see what happens if we keep going:

One of the shutters was broken and dangled crookedly, and dandelions populated the yard. Half the tiles had fallen from the roof. They lay scattered about the porch. Three of the windows were shattered. Paint was peeling from the walls. The whole structure listed as though drunk. Weeds choked the driveway.

Here we're trying to create a house in your head that looks identical to the one in ours. Not only is it unnecessary, it's counterproductive. If we'd kept writing you'd probably have stopped reading. (We stopped writing because it stopped being fun. We are in an honest mood.) The writer must allow readers to create their own imagery, and must give them just enough clues to point them in the right direction.

And here's the real magic: if you allow your readers to populate *your* story with *their* experiences, you benefit from the emotional boost those experiences bring with them. Everyone has seen a tumbledown house. Let your readers insert one from their own memory galleries.

Imagine a car salesman making you assemble the vehicle in his showroom before you're allowed to drive it home. Reading works much the same way: you not only have to buy the book, you have to form the images yourself. As a writer it's your job to ensure readers do the work, assemble the imagery in their own heads, put in enough effort to earn *your* royalty payment. Just make sure they have all the parts they need. Consider:

Susan's hair was long and straight and she wore knee-high boots.

If that's all we have to work with, we don't know what *kind* of picture to form of Susan (in the dealer showroom, we don't know what kind of car to assemble). Is she a schoolgirl? A hippie? A prostitute? Hopefully the context will let us know, but the description alone doesn't.

We recently read a submission in which the spouse didn't just run off with another man, she ran off with a fertilizer salesman. Wonderful! A fertilizer salesman who wore bow ties and drove a Fiat? Maybe, it depends on the context— and, as we said earlier, your own experience. You have to know when to stop.

We recently read a submission that opened with the major character sitting in a rocking chair, and the writer taking pains to inform us what kind of wood the rocking chair was made of. As we read further we waited to see how the species of wood mattered to the story. Of course it didn't.

The first 126 words of "Paul's Case" by Willa Cather deserve a close look:

It was Paul's afternoon to appear before the faculty of the Pittsburgh High School to account for his various misdemeanors. He had been suspended a week ago, and his father had called at the Principal's office and confessed his perplexity about his son. Paul entered the faculty room suave and smiling. His clothes were a trifle outgrown, and the tan velvet on the collar of his open overcoat was frayed and worn; but for all that there was something of a dandy about him, and he wore an opal pin in his neatly knotted black four-in-hand, and a red carnation in his buttonhole. This latter adornment the faculty somehow felt was not properly significant of the contrite spirit befitting a boy under the ban of suspension.

Lots of detail here, but it all serves a purpose and we're curious about Paul. Is the way he dresses authentic, or did he dress that way for the faculty? It remains to be seen. We can already guess he has little regard for the faculty, and we'll read further to learn what happens during the meeting. And that's the point: *we'll read further*. The modifiers you employ must serve a purpose. If you tell us Paul's collar is frayed there should be a reason we need to know it: in this case because he's appearing before the faculty and trying to make a specific impression. If you tell us what kind of wood the rocking chair is made of, the guy sitting in it might probably ought to be the lumberjack who cut down the tree.

The details contained in the first 103 words of *The Namesake* by Jhumpa Lahiri introduce a food motif without delay and make us hungry:

On a sticky August evening two weeks before her due date, Ashima Ganguli stands in the kitchen of a Central Square apartment, combining Rice Krispies and Planters peanuts and chopped red onion in a bowl. She adds salt, lemon juice, thin slices of green chili pepper, wishing there were mustard oil to pour into the mix. Ashima has been consuming this concoction throughout her pregnancy, a humble approximation of the snack sold for pennies on Calcutta sidewalks and on railway platforms throughout India, spilling from newspaper cones. Even now that there is barely space inside her, it is the one thing she craves.

Observe how Jonathan Franzen describes his high school principal in *The Discomfort Zone*:

Mr. Knight was a red-haired, red-bearded, Nordic-looking giant. He had a sideways, shambling way of walking, with frequent pauses to hitch up his pants, and he stood with the stooped posture of a man who spent his days listening to smaller people.

Is there anything else you really need to know about Mr. Knight?

Detail is tricky. In general, keep the old adage in mind that "less is more." Until, of course, less is too little. Many of the calories you burn writing should be expended worrying about how much detail to share.

*

The rules are somewhat different for poetry. Much of poetry is all about the details, and a word in a poem generally carries a heavier load than one in a story or essay. Still, if every leaf is green, if every wind is brisk, we yawn and skip to the next submission.

You've all heard the advice: use adjectives and adverbs sparingly. Follow that advice. As the late poet and professor Thomas Lux said, "There's a difference between writing poetically and writing poetry." Consider the following three lines:

Sweet voice, sweet lips, soft hand, and softer breast,
Warm breath, light whisper, tender semi-tone,
Bright eyes, accomplished shape, and languorous waist!

No one would write such stuff, you say, and to tell you the truth, it makes us queasy too. But this is a trick example, because, again, the rules are somewhat different for poetry. These lines come from "The day is gone, and all its sweets are gone!" by John Keats, who probably knew more about poetry than we do (but who might well adopt a different style today). Obey the rules at your own peril.

When we tell aspiring writers that, say, the color of the coffee cup on the breakfast table is irrelevant, and such details make us question whether the story is *about* the coffee cup, the aspiring writers invariably respond, "But that's the particular coffee cup in my mind, so I have to share its color with the reader." No, you don't. If you can cut an adjective or adverb, you should. If the piece suffers for the deletion, put it back. For example, consider the first line of "The Silken Tent" by Robert Frost:

She is as in a field a silken tent

Now take out "silken" and listen to what remains.

There's a secret society of writers devoted to eliminating adjectives and adverbs from the English language*. Though we respect their fervor, we find it helpful to think of adjectives and adverbs as jewelry. If the lady is pretty enough (if your paragraph is strong enough) a solitary diamond will do. Don't load the poor girl down with ornaments.

*There could be. Who can say for sure? We are in a playful mood.

We'll leave you with one final example, "When You Are Old" by William Butler Yeats. Count the number of modifiers; they're so skillfully placed we glide through them without protest. The poem consists of exactly 100 words:

When you are old and grey and full of sleep,
And nodding by the fire, take down this book,
And slowly read, and dream of the soft look
Your eyes had once, and of their shadows deep;

How many loved your moments of glad grace,
And loved your beauty with love false or true,
But one man loved the pilgrim soul in you,
And loved the sorrows of your changing face;

And bending down beside the glowing bars,
Murmur, a little sadly, how Love fled
And paced upon the mountains overhead
And hid his face amid a crowd of stars.

What more can you ask of a lover but that he love the pilgrim soul in you, and the sorrows of your changing face?

You're now fully equipped to pass the following test: In Wendell Berry's poem "The Peace of Wild Things" (poemhunter.com/poem/the-peace-of-wild-things), why "wood drake" rather than "ducks?"

Get to the Point

If you haven't read "The Metamorphosis" by Franz Kafka, at least you've heard of its famous first line:

As Gregor Samsa awoke one morning from uneasy dreams he found himself transformed in his bed into a gigantic insect.

Maybe you've read *The Bridge of San Luis Rey* by Thornton Wilder, which won the Pulitzer Prize. It begins with:

On Friday noon, July the twentieth, 1714, the finest bridge in all Peru broke and precipitated five travelers into the gulf below.

Not all stories can get to the point so quickly, nor should they, but every sentence you write should serve a purpose. And although the longer the story is, the more will be forgiven, your first 100 words had better not squander a single word. Contrast the previous examples with the next one:

I read about it in the paper, in the subway, on my way to work. I read it, and I couldn't believe it, and I read it again. Then perhaps I just stared at it, at the newsprint spelling out his name, spelling out the story. I stared at it in the swinging lights of the subway car, and in the faces and bodies of the people, and in my own face, trapped in the darkness which roared outside.

These first 79 words of "Sonny's Blues" by James Baldwin don't tell us much of anything. Let's keep reading:

It was not to be believed and I kept telling myself that, as I walked from the subway station to the high school. And at the same time I couldn't doubt it. I was scared, scared for Sonny. He became real to me again. A great block of ice got settled in my belly and kept melting there slowly all day long, while I taught my classes algebra.

Okay, now we know, if we didn't already from the title, the story concerns a person named Sonny, and the narrator is an algebra teacher. We still don't know what the story is about. Let's keep going:

It was a special kind of ice. It kept melting, sending trickles of ice water all up and down my veins, but it never got less. Sometimes it hardened and seemed to expand until I felt my guts were going to come spilling out or that I was going to choke or scream. This would always be at a moment when I was remembering some specific thing Sonny had once said or done.

Have you determined what the story is about? A visiting alien, ignorant of our habit of meandering into stories, might guess this one's got something to do with how water crystallizes at its freezing point. Continuing:

When he was about as old as the boys in my classes his face had been bright and open, there was a lot of copper in it; and he'd had wonderfully direct brown eyes, and a great gentleness and privacy. I wondered what he looked like now.

We're getting a picture of Sonny. We still don't know what's going on. Until the next line:

He had been picked up, the evening before, in a raid on an apartment downtown, for peddling and using heroin.

Finally, after 287 words. We love Baldwin and would nominate him for sainthood, but we wonder if the story would improve if it opened with the arrest, whether we would care more about both Sonny and the narrator, and care sooner, if the first 38 words were:

I read about it in the paper, in the subway, on my way to work. My little brother Sonny had been picked up, the evening before, in a raid on an apartment downtown, for peddling and using heroin.

But hang on. Sonny is the algebra teacher's little brother? Baldwin couldn't have shoehorned that tidbit into the first 287 words? Now read what follows the arrest notice:

I couldn't believe it: but what I mean by that is that I couldn't find any room for it anywhere inside me. I had kept it outside me for a long time. I hadn't wanted to know. I had had suspicions, but I didn't name them, I kept putting them away.

Pretty much everything the writer wanted us to know prior to telling us what the story is about, he summarized afterwards. At this point you're thinking one of two things. Either "Who the hell are you to criticize an icon?" or "I shouldn't feel so bad about my own story openings, thank you very much." Fair enough on the first. As for the second, nice try, sorry, you're not James Baldwin.

We know from sharing this example with beta readers that they're divided into two camps, one favoring a more direct approach and one favoring the original version. An editor defended the latter position this way: "I think the passage works because what Baldwin is trying to do is create the slow-build ache of dread that sits heavy in the middle of your belly and seeps through your veins to your extremities. And then after that long, agonizing deal of a long, agonizing dread you get the gut punch of the reveal. He makes the reader feel what the narrator is feeling."

Decide for yourself. Writing, like life, consists of choices and consequences. The choices are all yours.

There are several reasons we hesitate to get to the point when we begin writing. One is because we want to provide the reader as much background as possible before the action begins. Usually it's best to integrate the background as the story progresses. Consider:

Artillery flashes illuminated the horizon, followed seconds later by the rolling thunder of exploding shells. The battle drew closer. The night was rent by the cries of dying men up and down the line. An enemy soldier approached my foxhole, observed that I was wounded, and fixed his bayonet.

Nothing wrong with this, but let's begin with storytelling and integrate the background:

As the enemy soldier approached, artillery flashes illuminated the horizon behind him, followed seconds later by the rolling thunder of exploding shells. The night was rent by the cries of dying men up and down the line. The soldier stopped before my foxhole, observed that I was wounded, and fixed his bayonet. The battle had finally reached me.

Whether the difference is subtle, as above, or you have pages of world-building to share, get into the story first. It's where the reader wants to be. Observe one way Hemingway could have begun "Old Man at the Bridge:"

There was a pontoon bridge across the river and carts, trucks, and men, women and children were crossing it. The mule-drawn carts staggered up the steep bank from the bridge with soldiers helping push against the spokes of the wheels. The trucks ground up and away heading out of it all and the peasants plodded along in the ankle deep dust. An old man with steel rimmed spectacles and very dusty clothes sat by the side of the road. He sat there without moving. He was too tired to go any further.

Compare that with how Hemingway actually began the story. By bringing the character in first, rather than his setting, we see the setting from the character's perspective:

An old man with steel rimmed spectacles and very dusty clothes sat by the side of the road. There was a pontoon bridge across the river and carts, trucks, and men, women and children were crossing it. The mule-drawn carts staggered up the steep bank from the bridge with soldiers helping push against the spokes of the wheels. The trucks ground up and away heading out of it all and the peasants plodded along in the ankle deep dust. But the old man sat there without moving. He was too tired to go any further.

Another reason we hesitate to get to the point is we want to build suspense. Yet suspense is something readers feel as they anticipate what comes *next*. They can't anticipate what comes next until they know what comes *first*.

He couldn't believe it was happening to him again. He thought the previous time should have been the last. But here he was, facing it yet again, and this time it didn't look like it was going to end well, either.

We get lots of these. Do you feel any suspense? Maybe this would work deeper in the story—maybe—but it fails in the first 100 words. *Start* with story, *integrate* background, *build* suspense.

Astute readers might point out that Ian Anderson's "The Odd Job," quoted earlier, breaks the rule:

I'm sitting at the kitchen table with my Saturday afternoon tea when Georgie comes in through the back.

He's talking even before he closes the door. "Wait until you hear this one. You are not going to believe this one."

But notice the narrator is in the same position we're in; he must also wait to hear what "this one" is all about.

Another reason we hesitate is we feel leaping in is too abrupt, and therefore some scrollwork is necessary. New writers are generally forgiven this tactic, especially by astute critique partners who know where to draw the line: "Your story really begins *here.*" Scrollwork is parasitic; it clings to the front of storytelling and disguises itself as a natural part of the writing. Consider the following opening sentence, variations of which are waiting their turn in the slush as we speak:

The two incidents seemed incompatible.

Harmless enough, you may say, but so are many parasites. All it accomplishes is a delay in the storytelling. If you want us to care about the two incidents and their incompatibility, first tell us what the two incidents are, then *show* us why they're incompatible. We'll forgive, for the moment, using the word "seemed" in this context, and leave the reason for mentioning it as an exercise. We are in an instructive mood.

In the opening paragraph of *Lit* by Mary Karr the narrator gets to the point in the first sentence. She also provides an impressive amount of background information in just 70 words:

Age seventeen, stringy-haired and halter-topped, weighing in the high-double digits and unhindered by a high school diploma, I showed up at the Pacific Ocean, ready to seek my fortune with a truck full of extremely stoned surfers. My family, I thought them to be, for such was my quest—a family I could stand alongside pondering the sea. We stood as the blue water surged toward us in six-foot coils.

One of Kurt Vonnegut's Rules for Writers is "Give your readers as much information as possible as soon as possible. To heck with suspense. Readers should have such complete understanding of what is going on, where and why, that they could finish the story themselves, should cockroaches eat the last few pages."

Agree or disagree, either way pay careful attention to how quickly you get to the point, and have a good reason for every speed bump you construct.

Consider the opening of Everything I Never Told You, by Celeste Ng:

Lydia is dead. But they don't know this yet. 1977, May 3, six thirty in the morning, no one knows anything but this innocuous fact: Lydia is late for breakfast.

A lesser writer might open with "They don't yet know what happened." We see that every day in the slush. Ng gets to the point: "Lydia is dead." The "late for breakfast" follow-up intrigues us; we not only want to know how Lydia died, we want to know the consequences. Rewrite your openings until they accomplish as much. Rewrite them over and over, if necessary. Rewrite them until *you* can't wait to read what follows.

*

You hear it everywhere: don't begin with the weather. Mind you, it's only a misdemeanor when committed by aspiring writers, but whenever frontline readers encounter clouds at the top of a story they immediately think, "Oh no, not another one." Ask yourself weather (ha ha) that's what you want your editor to think when she begins reading.

Right now some of you are rummaging around for examples of great stories that begin with the weather, and we're going to preempt you. "The Lottery" by Shirley Jackson is universally acknowledged to be one of the most influential stories written in English. There's a reason for Jackson's felonious behavior: she's contrasting the pleasantness of the day with the horrible event about to follow.

The morning of June 27th was clear and sunny, with the fresh warmth of a full-summer day; the flowers were blossoming profusely and the grass was richly green. The people of the village began to gather in the square...

Jackson devotes only 28 words to the weather; she then dives immediately into story. If you can write as effectively we'll forgive your roiling clouds and pounding rain.

A surprisingly high percentage of stories and poems we receive begins with sunlight streaming through curtains, complete with dust motes. It's just another species of scrollwork. So are dream sequences; no matter how useful they are, or you think they are, they've devolved into eye-rolling trope. Cut such stuff. Start your story at the beginning of your story. Don't test the editor's patience by spending the first 100 words ramping up.

*

Save movie scenes for screenwriting, unless that's the atmosphere you're trying to create. Incidentally, don't try to create that atmosphere. You're writing a story or poem or essay, not a movie. This is what we're talking about:

The clock reads precisely half past eight. The room is quiet but for a distant wailing, perhaps a small child on another floor of the house. Through the rain-streaked window can be seen headlights winding their way slowly up the dark hill.

We see too many of these, and they don't belong in our slush pile. Sorry to be blunt, but if you write with Camera rather than Quill you should send your stuff to Steven Spielberg instead. He knows what to do with it.

Don't let all this admonishment get you down. We know what you're going through; we're writers too. Sometimes it feels like you're standing in front of editors in your underwear, waiting to be judged. Just "write drunk, edit sober." Write with as much reckless abandon as you wish, share all the crazy, wonderful things in your head, and don't let Perfect interfere with Plenty Good Enough. Then edit judiciously, like a nitpicking mother-in-law invited to Thanksgiving dinner. And remember, all writers must stand in their underwear before their *readers*. The job of an editor—and this book—is to make you look better before you step in front of them.

Master Your Craft

Almost everything you need to know about craft is in Strunk and White. Almost. And we are in a generous mood.

Cut the clichés. The rule is simple: if you've heard an expression before, like *His life was a rollercoaster*, purge it from your expression grab-bag, even if the life of the knucklehead in question is, indeed, a rollercoaster.

Abstain from hyperbole. For example, *Her brain overflowed with confusion*. As you read your work, ask yourself whether what you're describing is truly possible. Hearts don't really "pound." Things don't actually "fill" the air.

Simplicity is an underrated virtue. Instead of *She stretched her lips across her teeth* please just say *She smiled*.

Try not to have your characters sigh or purse their lips; all the other characters in all the other stories we get are doing it, and it's beginning to weird us out.

Don't have your characters *proceed* to do something, just have them do it. Don't have your narrators *remember* what happened, just have them relate it.

Don't get lost in the Woulds. Compare the following two texts and decide for yourself which is cleaner:

I spent the summer writing a novel. I would get up at dawn, fuel myself with coffee, and pound the keyboard. The characters would resist my efforts to comprehend their motives; I would feel them pull away from me. But I'd stick with them, often until late, until they'd reveal their secrets or I'd collapse with fatigue.

I spent the summer writing a novel. I got up at dawn, fueled myself with coffee, and pounded the keyboard. The characters resisted my efforts to comprehend their motives; I felt them pull away from me. But I stuck with them, often until late, until they revealed their secrets or I collapsed with fatigue.

Word-vermin to avoid in the absence of a compelling reason include firmament, moonbeam, sunray, waft, slake, sashay, abyss, tummy, and LOL. A disconcerting number of opening sentences in the slush contains crude language. Although the title of this book isn't *The First Word*, if you begin your story with a crude word we'll decline to read the next 99 you offer us. Likewise most references to bodily fluids, including the inexplicably ubiquitous butt sweat.

Varmint words that have been illegal in creative writing at least since the Ptolemaic Dynasty include 'ere, o'er, ne'er, alas, hark, yonder, hither, and thither.

If you use the word "cuz" we'll take away your birthday. If you name your protagonist "Deke" we'll tell everyone you voted for Sarah Palin.

Once upon a time, writers opened stories with "Once upon a time." They stopped when we turned off their hot water.

Poets should get together and figure out why so many are writing about absinthe. Which reminds us, why doesn't pumpernickel bread get its fair shake? We put it to you.

Do a document search for rodents like really, very, every, suddenly, began, started, finally, then, and that, and challenge each appearance. For example change "The economy began to prosper" to "The economy prospered" and "She knew that he was wrong" to "She knew he was wrong."

Please stop saying *begs the question* when you mean *raises the question*. Just because CNN anchors do it doesn't make it right, it just makes them illiterate. To beg a question is to commit a logical fallacy.

Eliminate as many present participles as you can. They're nasty little parasites that are highly skilled at camouflage.

For example change *No one was speaking* to *No one spoke.* If necessary do a document search for "ing."

Poetry and song lyrics are different genres. If your poem sounds like the pop song "Seasons in the Sun," you need a bass player, not a literary journal.

One of the fastest ways to lose an editor's interest in the first 100 words is through grammatical errors. It's okay to accidentally write *though* when you mean *thought* if it happens deep in the piece; spell check won't catch such mistakes. (We expect someone will find something in this book and say, "*J'accuse!*") But not in the first 100 words. When errors appear there, the impression is one of sloppiness. Proofread your work thoroughly. If you make more serious errors, like apostrophe's denoting plural noun's, you might be in the wrong field.

With rare exception, dialogue tags should consist of a pronoun and the word "said." Challenge each one of your dialogue tags and remove them if the conversation flows satisfactorily without them. Compare:

"I'm going to give you some advice," Wilbur declared.

Millicent looked up from her knitting. "And what would that be?" she inquired.

with:

"I'm going to give you some advice," Wilbur said.

Millicent looked up from her knitting. "And what would that be?"

One peeve of ours is one we like to call "square dancing with dialogue tags." Here's an example: *"No, I won't iron your shirt," Nancy announced, turning away from her husband, storming into the living room, watching over her shoulder to see if he would follow.* Do-si-do your partner, now allemande left! We'll leave fixing the sentence as an exercise. Don't try to say too much in one breath.

*

Bad metaphors and similes are distracting, to say the least, and the worst of them come across as unintended comedy: *Sweat trickled down his leg like a warm, wet serpent. The sun's glare followed her like a lovesick candle.*

Don't use anything you've heard before. Don't use it even if you only suspect it's been used before. For example we see a lot of comparisons to Sisyphus (life is hard; we get it). You won't necessarily be rejected for such misdemeanors, but be prepared to cut them.

The opening couplet in "Turbulence" by Maggie Smith (lascauxreview.com/turbulence) is a simile:

The sky shakes us
like a shoe with a stone inside.

First, it's appropriate; it illustrates passengers in an airliner during turbulence and doesn't reach too far out of its domain (like comparing sweat to serpents). Even "shoe" suggests transportation. True, it exaggerates, but that's the nature of metaphor. It paints a vivid picture with great efficiency, which is what metaphors are employed to do.

Would you compare two lovers to the legs of a drafting compass? Think before you answer. John Donne did so, in "A Valediction: Forbidding Mourning," with surprising effect:

And though it in the center sit,
Yet when the other far doth roam,
It leans, and hearkens after it,
And grows erect, as that comes home.

Tony Hoagland, in "A Color of the Sky," describes a "little dogwood losing its mind," and turns metaphor into art:

overflowing with blossomfoam,
like a sudsy mug of beer;

like a bride ripping off her clothes,
dropping snow white petals to the ground in clouds

Mary Oliver wrote, "A poem that is composed without the sweet and correct formalities of language, which are what sets it apart from the dailiness of ordinary writing, is doomed. It will not fly. It will be raucous and sloppy—the work of an amateur." Pay attention to metaphors and similes as you read other poets and writers, and decide for yourself which work, which don't, and which straddle the crevasse between. They'll make or break you as a writer.

*

Opening your story with dialogue is fraught with danger. Fraught, we tell you! That doesn't mean it's wrong, or even that you should avoid it, just that it's hard to pull off—because there's no context. We don't know anything about the characters speaking and therefore struggle to care about, or even understand, the conversation:

"Don't push me," he said. "I need to manage this in my own time. The clients should come first."
"Our lawyers advise us to act now," she said.
"Can't we work this out privately? Do the courts really need to get involved?"
"I'll be down the hall. Call me when you've made up your mind. But don't take too long."

On the other hand, here are the first 44 words of "The Veldt" by Ray Bradbury. If you engage the reader you can open your story any way you like, including with dialogue—fraught with danger though it may be.

"George, I wish you'd look at the nursery."
"What's wrong with it?"
"I don't know."
"Well, then."
"I just want you to look at it, is all, or call a psychologist in to look at it."
"What would a psychologist want with a nursery?"

P.S. Notice the absence of dialogue tags?

*

Vary your sentence lengths to retain reader interest and evoke reader response. Consider this paragraph from the essay "How I Write" by Bertrand Russell, who won the Nobel Prize in Literature in 1950:

Very gradually I have discovered ways of writing with a minimum of worry and anxiety. When I was young each fresh piece of serious work used to seem beyond my powers. I would fret myself into a nervous state from fear that it was never going to come right. I would make one unsatisfying attempt after another. In the end I would have to discard them all. At last I found that such fumbling attempts were a waste of time. It appeared that after first contemplating a book on some subject I needed a period of subconscious incubation. The period of incubation could not be hurried. If anything it was impeded by deliberate thinking. Sometimes I would find that I had made a mistake. I would find that I could not write the book I had had in mind. But often I was more fortunate. Having planted the problem in my subconsciousness, it would germinate underground. Then suddenly the solution emerged with blinding clarity. It only remained to write down what had appeared as if in a revelation.

The Russell fans reading this are presently scampering off to call their lawyers, because we cheated. That isn't how Russell composed the paragraph. But we wanted you to read a monotonous version first, for the sake of contrast. Here's how he actually put it:

Very gradually I have discovered ways of writing with a minimum of worry and anxiety. When I was young each fresh piece of serious work used to seem to me for a time—perhaps a long time—to be beyond my powers. I would fret myself into a nervous state from fear that it was never going to come right. I would make one unsatisfying attempt after another, and in the end have to discard them all. At last I found that such fumbling attempts were a waste of time. It appeared that after first contemplating a book on some subject, and after giving serious preliminary attention to it, I needed a period of subconscious incubation which could not be hurried and was, if anything, impeded by deliberate thinking.

Sometimes I would find, after a time, that I had made a mistake, and that I could not write the book I had had in mind. But often I was more fortunate. Having, by a time of very intense concentration, planted the problem in my subconsciousness, it would germinate underground until, suddenly, the solution emerged with blinding clarity, so that it only remained to write down what had appeared as if in a revelation.

Feel the difference varying the tempo makes in your reading experience? The effect is deliberate; the author didn't achieve it by accident. Notice especially how the final sentence, the longest in the paragraph, stretches into a crescendo, and that the sentence immediately prior is the shortest in the paragraph. Russell, whose greatest contributions were to philosophy and mathematics, won the Nobel Prize in literature.

To round out this part of the book, before we get to the business end of things, here are a few opening paragraphs that made the editors of *The Lascaux Review* want to read more:

It was Rocket Night at our daughter's elementary school, the night when parents, students, and administrators gather to place the least-liked child in a rocket and shoot him into the stars. Last year we placed Laura Jackson into the capsule, a short, squat girl known for the limp dresses that hung crookedly on her body. The previous year we'd sent off a boy from

India whose name none of us could remember. —Alexander Weinstein, "Rocket Night" (lascauxreview.com/rocket-night).

One day he was cock-of-the-walk, full of jokes and juice, strumming his guitar, waxing the big fins on his red Chevy, knowing another woman in the biblical sense. The next day woebegone, collapsing like a library on fire and the water hose too short. —Janice D. Soderling, "Adultery" (lascauxreview.com/adultery).

My first girlfriend was Catholic, and thought no one would know she was a lesbian if she kept up a great manicure. A year of Bonnie, her legs sticking lightly to my cheeks. A year of Bonnie's downy hair reaching like the tail of a star up to her belly button. Of secret handholding under the Calculus desks. Her blood ran so hot, to touch her was to turn her into a fogged window, a pink lampshade in a red light district. She covered her eyes with her arm the whole time I was in her bed. —Lori Nevole, "White Chrysanthemums" (lascauxreview.com/white-chrysanthemums).

Act Professionally

All that matters is the writing, you might argue, and ultimately you'd be right. But imagine showing up on a blind date with something dangling from your nose. You could hit it off and even get lucky, but it probably won't be love at first sight.

Use Times New Roman, 12 point, no justification, no colors, no decorations, no drop caps, nothing bold, nothing fancy, unless instructed otherwise. But it looks boring, you say. Good. All that matters is the writing, remember? And besides, you can't improve writing with anything other than better writing.

Understand that according to the bylaws of the Right Honorable Order of Literary Editors (Lodge 235) we're not allowed to read anything written in ALL CAPS, not even your book titles—unless you write in crayon, in which case your work will likely be rejected for other "technical" reasons.

Since the advent of what used to be called "desktop publishing" there's been a trend to make the submission look as much as possible like the writer envisions the final published result will look. Don't do that.

Turn off track changes and the comment function. To be safe, paste your text into a new document before submitting it, because the mark-ups sometimes appear on the Submittable interface, as well as some email interfaces, even when the functions have been turned off. If we witness Eunice, your beta reader, rescue you from confusing "prostate" with "prostrate," that nightmare you have of appearing naked in front of the class will have come true. (Things are getting a little chipper here, but what can we say? We are in a frolicsome mood.)

Copyright notices make you look like an amateur. As do statements like "all rights reserved." Your work is automatically copyrighted when you create it. If you offer us "first North American serial rights" you must be referencing guidance from the 1970s, or guidance that got its guidance from guidance from the 1970s. WGA registration numbers are not only unnecessary, they're unsettlingly weird; if you fear we're going to rip you off, why send us your work?

Like all reasonable editors, we accept simultaneous submissions, so we understand if you goof up and forget to change the salutation, or when you tell *The Lascaux Review*, "I think my poem would be perfect for *The Paris Review*."

Nevertheless, professionalism is about attending to the details, and if instead of *The Paris Review* you address it to *The East Bumblefuck Review*, we now know where we stand in your hierarchy of literary journals.

We shouldn't have to say this, but singling out characters as black, Jewish, etc., triggers an alarm, especially if the rascally WASPs go unlabeled. If you introduce female characters by describing their looks, do the same for the male characters, and in either case, have a reason.

Don't ever unload your drawer on a journal. Send one submission at a time. Most editors, when they see as many as a dozen pieces in a row from the same writer (yes, it happens, regularly), will brace themselves for an onslaught and end up skimming most of them—if they look at them at all. You don't want to be a source of pain to your prospective publisher. Also, most journals using Submittable have a monthly limit to the number of free submissions they can receive. If you shotgun us you'll crash us into our ceilings, and we'll want to come over there and sit on you.

Be polite. Some writers want to know why their submissions were rejected, and it's a fair question. We respond whenever politely asked. But then we always duck and cringe, because we're honest, and honesty can be brutal, and sometimes the writer fires back, telling us our perspective is only an opinion (of course it is), and our opinion is wrong (it may well be). Also, that *The East Bumblefuck*

Review already accepted the piece in question (congratulations), therefore our constituent atoms could be more usefully employed in the manufacture of cabbage fertilizer (please wait until we're dead).

Most editors will tell you they don't have the time to provide feedback. We suppose it depends on the editor. We assure you none have the *desire*, because the best they can hope for is not to be yelled at. For the record, the only proper response to criticism of your writing, any criticism at all, if you respond at all, is "Thank you," followed by a period and nothing else at all.

Follow the Instructions

There are people who follow instructions, there are people who ignore them. The latter will never convert to the former. It's a law of cosmology. For a few months in 2019 we conducted an experiment at *The Lascaux Review*. We asked submitters to note in their submission that they'd read the guidelines. One in fifteen complied.

This doesn't necessarily mean only one in fifteen read the guidelines—some no doubt had submitted before, and understandably didn't read them again, some merely forgot to add the note when they submitted a week later—but it does suggest the majority of submitters don't bother themselves with such trifling matters. At the Submittable portal we explained "Title" meant title of the work, yet we still received submissions in which the writer entered Mr., Ms., Dr., etc., even though the instructions were *right next to the box.*

Here's the irony. This passage, the passage you're reading now, constitutes guidance. Those of you who don't follow guidance won't follow this guidance either. The nonfollowers of guidance reading this guidance will never stop not-following guidance.

Here's the consequence. Remember what we said earlier about Diogenes? If you ignore the guidelines you make it easy for us to reject you. We speak for all editors, everywhere, dead or alive or transitioning one direction or the other: follow the damn submission guidelines.

Apparently most submissions nowadays arrive via market listings like Duotrope. There's nothing wrong with using such listings, they're assets to the industry. But you have to visit the journal too.

In a former career we reviewed thousands of job applications and interviewed hundreds of candidates. A third of the candidates knew nothing at all about the company— they'd done no homework—and some couldn't even spell its name correctly. A few insisted God had chosen them for the job. We answered that God had said precious little to us about it. Granted, we're getting off-track here, but we are in a squirrely mood.

The First 100 Words of the Bio

The bio matters because most journals publish it with the piece, usually at the end, and thus it becomes part of the total presentation. It may come across as incongruous if it begins "Catherine raises gerbils, is only half-incarnated, and craves coconut milk when watching reruns of Gilligan's Island." If your bio needs rewriting you're stepping unnecessarily on a landmine by providing the editor with an obstacle to acceptance. If you leave the space blank, or you flippantly enter a solitary word like "Alive," you're forcing the editor to wonder what she's going to do about it, which is another obstacle to acceptance. If your bio makes you sound crazy you'll make the editor nervous, which is ... you know the drill.

We're looking for reasons to publish you. Don't provide reasons not to.

By "bio" we mean literary bio, and 100 words is all you need. It's not a CV, so don't list every accomplishment and publication. It's also not a place to get cute. When you read it out loud ask yourself, is this what you want us to know about you? That your cat's name is Fluffy? Listen:

Cindy Lou Scribbler's stories and poems have appeared in Great Unwashed Literary Journal, Bird Flu Quarterly, the anthology I'd Turn Back If I Were You, and elsewhere. Her debut novel is forthcoming from Wormy Apple Press. She has an MFA from Dunderhead University and reads for The East Bumblefuck Review.

That's it. That's all you need. The example above consists of fifty words. It's brief, third person, and relevant. If you're a Pulitzer finalist there's plenty of room left over to say so. Be honest, be modest. Someone with no publications might write something like this:

Cindy Lou Scribbler is an aspiring writer from Chicago. She graduated from Northwestern with a B.A. in English and participates in her local SFWA chapter.

That's all you have to say—srsly! If you're submitting a war story, by all means mention you served in Afghanistan. If it's an essay about new technologies in emergency health care, of course we want to know you drive an ambulance. Otherwise we don't care that your family moved to Pennsylvania when you were five, or that you currently split your time between Pittsburgh and The Catskills—which just informs us where you park your lawnmower and, respectively, your RV.

Be specific: the phrase "65 poems in 52 magazines" tells us nothing, at least not without examples. Save the number of states, countries, and continents you've visited for *National Geographic*. Don't supply links and invite us to learn all about you. Just tell us, briefly, what we ought to know.

Resist naming your pets, no matter how many other writers are getting away with it (every time you do so, a puppy dies). When it comes to prizes, list the ones you won, not the honorable mentions (it's the honorable thing to do). Be aware that of eight billion people on Earth, 7,999,999,999 have been nominated for a Pushcart Prize*. Uncountable hoards have been *Glimmer Train* finalists.

*Wilbur Crotchburn of Roanoke VA is still waiting.

Everyone loves the written word. Everyone has been reading and writing as far back as they can remember. Everyone wants world peace. Everyone was born and everyone was raised. Our cats are named Rusty and Blacky, just so you know.

*

You may have heard the advice that writers shouldn't admit they're unpublished, for fear of not being taken seriously. We understand the concern. We've sometimes found that writers are as reluctant to admit the piece we're publishing is their first as they are to admit their secret hobby is time travel. Especially since the Brooklyn Dodgers remain—to this day!—in Los Angeles. (Our lawyers insist we clarify that time travelers aren't responsible for the move to Los Angeles, only for failing to correct the error.)

Speaking for ourselves, discovering new talent is half the reason we got into this business. When a writer admits in her bio or cover letter that the piece in question would constitute her first publication, we at *The Lascaux Review* perk up and take notice. We're inclined to do our best, maybe break a rule or two, to get her in. We would only hope editors at sister journals feel the same way.

Bonus Stuff

We're going to step out of bounds here, because this section doesn't necessarily address the first 100 words of anything. We want to equip you as best we can to go as far as your talent will take you. And later we'll even have something to say about talent.

Some themes are tired, and the bar is so high you need to lower your expectations about publishing them. We're speaking of course about death in the family, and in general about anything everyone in the world experiences at one time or another. We call them "dying grandma stories." Unless the execution is brilliant, we're sorry, the answer will be no. Of course as a writer you have to write such pieces, you have to get them out of your system. You have to submit them too. Just don't get discouraged if they live out their lives in a drawer.

When submitting multiple poems or flash pieces—all in one document, right?—position your best one first. Faith and hope diminish as editors scroll.

If a scene isn't working, when you just can't get it right, the most common culprit, assuming the writer knows how to put one word in front of another, is an absence of conflict. It needn't be on a large scale; merely one character looking askance at another might do the job. Dialogue is often a lens to the deficiency:

"What would you like for breakfast?"
"Bacon and eggs."
"With orange juice?"
"Sure, orange juice would be great."
"And toast?"
"Yes, thank you."

Don't laugh. Or rather, do laugh, but this kind of writing is common in the slush, especially coming from fiction writers who believe their duty is to capture reality. Readers don't want reality. They get reality at their own breakfast tables.

You'll often hear the truism that character drives story. Fair enough. Conflict reveals character that drives story. Let's try that breakfast dialogue again:

"Hungry? Or are you too hung over to hold it down."
"I'm fine. Just give me some eggs."
"What's her name?"
"Whose name?"

"The reason you came stumbling home after midnight. Her name."
"I don't know what you're talking about."
"Of course not. You didn't know last Saturday morning, either."

Too much? Then scale it back. Conflict doesn't have to take the form of a battle:

"How would you like your eggs?"
"I don't know. Scrambled, I guess."
"You got home sort of late last night."
"So?"
"It's just that ... nothing. Forget I brought it up. Bacon?"
"If it's not too much trouble."

Used to be, anything longer than 8000 words was considered long. Now it's more like 5000, and many markets are frowning at pieces over 3000. The flash phenomenon (we used to call them "short shorts") is helping to drive the agenda. Poems, too, are getting shorter. Our journal still considers long pieces, but now more than ever, the longer your submission, the better it must be. Emerging writers should tackle short pieces to improve their chances of publication.

"You're telling us to conform!" you say. No, we're telling you why your stuff might not be getting through.

Find an honest crit partner. Find several if you can. You probably want to tell them to ease off the praise and bear down on the weaknesses. If you do this you join a minority of writers who authentically seek honest feedback. It's long been our experience that most writers, having brainstormed and sketched and drafted and redrafted and tweaked and polished before sharing their work, seek validation, not criticism.

We sympathize. Writing is work, and writing long projects can be arduous. You want the job to be done. What's going to separate you from the panhandlers, ruffians, and scallywags is simply recognizing that it's not done until it's published. Talented and, especially, honest crit partners should rank in your life at least as high as your extramarital lovers, maybe even as high as your massage therapist. Bring them Oreo Cookies and Châteauneuf-du-Pape.

And while we're here, the more you crit and help others with their work, the better writer you become. If you're in search of a priceless education, volunteer to read for a literary journal.

Plot and theme are beyond the scope of this book, but we can devote a hundred words or so to them. If you have trouble, just start with the following oversimplified formula and build from it as necessary:

a) A protagonist wants something. The more she wants it, the better for the story.

b) An obstacle prevents her from getting it. The more challenging the obstacle, the better for the story.

c) The plot is how the protagonist overcomes the obstacle, or fails to do so. The theme is how she changes as a result of the experience. The more significant the change, the better for the story.

Suffering from writer's block? It helps to write only in lower case and without paragraph indentations; doing so provides the look and feel of a draft and makes it easier to move things around, cut scrollwork, and perform other as-you-write editing tasks. If you change the font as well the piece will feel like someone else wrote it; you can take your work less seriously and kill your darlings without guilt.

When you kill your darlings, save the deleted text in a morgue file. You'll move forward secure in knowing they can be raised from the dead, if necessary.

Stick with the project, return to it day after day, even if you don't think you're getting anywhere. Log jams always, eventually, break free. When you get flowing again, when you're clickety-clacking again, *don't hold back.*

Be True to Yourself. Every creative obstacle you encounter as a writer is, one way or another, a consequence of ignoring this rule. Maxwell Perkins, the legendary editor of Hemingway, Fitzgerald, Wolfe, and many others, once wrote to Taylor Caldwell that "Editors are extremely fallible people, all of them. Don't put too much trust in them." He wrote to *The Yearling* author Marjorie Rawlings, "The publisher must not try to get a writer to fit the book to the conditions of the trade, etc. It must be the other way around."

That attitude may be extinct in New York publishing, but it's alive and cutting rugs in literary journals. Be True to Yourself. As Martín Espada wrote in "Advice to Young Poets,"

Never pretend
to be a unicorn
by sticking a plunger on your head

Wrapping Up

You never arrive. You never reach the level where you say, I'm good enough, I'm a professional, I can stop bothering with books like *The First 100 Words*. Even if you've begun to place stories, poems, or essays, you have to keep reaching for the next level. Identify a weakness in your writing and work to strengthen it.

The old adage "If it ain't broke, don't fix it" is the worst advice an artist can take. It's *always* broke.

How do you identify weaknesses in your writing? Listen to your guts. You've all made changes to your work you suspected were wrong, changes a teacher or editor or crit partner demanded. Cling to that feeling: you knew the changes were wrong because your guts told you so. When the changes are right, you know it for the same reason.

There eventually comes a time when you're no longer tentative about your writing. You have a voice, a sense of style, an ear that is tuned to the complexities of creative writing. The pen in your hand obeys you, not the people around you, not even your writing idols. That sense of confidence has no external source. It comes from within. Like all the Whos down in Whoville singing on Christmas morning, it starts out low, then it starts to grow.

You first notice something's changing when you draft a scene or stanza that sticks with you the rest of the day. When you read it again the next day, it doesn't suck. The way you know something is good enough is when it fails to make you blush when you read it again after having placed yourself at a distance.

Because doubt manifests itself in your gut. Doubt doesn't let go. Doubt can't be silenced by covering your ears and chanting, "Nyah, nyah, nyah." If you experience doubt about your writing, if you fear it might not be accomplishing what you want it to, it isn't. If you remotely suspect it sucks, it does.

That's how you identify weaknesses in your writing: you listen to the doubt in your guts.

You all know that success is the result of hard work. Well, talent is the result of hard work on craft, i.e., on strengthening weaknesses. As for luck, it's nothing more than the result of hard work on opportunity, i.e., taking calculated risks.

Take risks. Sir Ken Robinson said, "If you're not prepared to be wrong, you'll never come up with anything original."

We've known a number of talented writers who we felt were on the verge of breaking through when they quit. The truth is, you fail *only* when you quit, and the hill is often steepest near the crest. Creative writing is a buyer's market. For every open slot there are other writers, often many writers, vying for it. You treat the problem the same way you treat job applications: when one myopic editor turns you down, submit to another. Those talented writers who quit before they broke through couldn't see the crest of the hill.

It's there. It's right there. It's right in front of you. If you're truly passionate about writing you won't quit, and you don't need people like us to urge you not to. But you do need to know you're not alone, that journal editors understand what you're going through, that they're almost always writers too, that they open the next file, and the one after, and every submission that comes their way, hoping for a chance to shout, to bang their fists on the desk, to bask in validation of the hours they've spent searching for gems in the gravel. To celebrate the discovery on the screen before them.

That's what we do. It's why we got into the business.

Winston Churchill said, "Never give in, never give in, never, never, never, never—in nothing, great or small, large or petty—never give in except to convictions of honor and good sense."

Be that writer. Be the writer who keeps returning to the keyboard. Be the writer who listens to criticism, who always reaches for the next level. Be the writer who thanks the myopic editor who rejects her, then kicks the furniture, then apologizes to the furniture, *then* returns to work and rewrites the piece and submits it to another editor, hopefully one with better taste. Be the writer who writes for herself, who is true to herself, but is also aware of readers leaning over her shoulder. Be the writer who understands we're all in this together, and the competition isn't other writers, it's television and movies and video games. And cake. Be the writer who participates in the writing community, who gives back as much as she takes.

The community is here for you. Legions of other writers are happy to share advice. If you don't hear their voices it's because you don't raise your hand and ask for help. No writer or editor with a heart will ignore the question, "How can I make this better?" You're not alone. If you have a breakdown, send us an email. We are in a loving mood.

—Stephen Parrish, with the editors of *The Lascaux Review*

Bibliography

The Elements of Style, by William Strunk Jr. and E. B. White, Macmillan, 1959 (and several editions since). The definitive work on the subject, and almost the only how-to book you need. Almost.

The Geek's Guide to the Writing Life, by Stephanie Vanderslice, Bloomsbury, 2018. A friendly and comprehensive introduction to the field, with links to a broad range of resources. Dr. Vanderslice runs the MFA program at the University of Central Arkansas.

For additional resources see lascauxreview.com/resources.